To Bill & M
Congratulations on
a good thing going for
all these years!!
Tonia Caspersen Crouch

Texas Twosomes: Married for Life

By
Donia Caspersen Crouch

Photographs by
Colleen Dilworth Stroup

Published in the United States of America
By Eakin Press
A Division of Sunbelt Media, Inc.
P.O. Box 90159
Austin, Texas 78709
Email: eakinpub@sig.net

2 3 4 5 6 7 8 9

ISBN 1-57168-233-3

Library of Congress Cataloging-in-Publication Data

Crouch, Donia Caspersen.
Texas twosomes: married for life / by Donia Caspersen Crouch:
photographs by Colleen Dilworth Stroup
p. cm.
ISBN 1-57168-233-3
1. Marriage—Texas—Case studies. I. Title.
HQ555.T4C78 1998
306.81'09764—dc21 98-33589
CIP

On the Cover

The cover couple is Donia Caspersen and Bob Dilworth, the mother of the writer and the father of the photographer. Donia and her husband Charlie had been married for forty-two years when he died in 1987. Bob and Susie Dilworth were married for thirty-eight years before she died of cancer ten years ago. Big believers in lasting marriages, Bob and Donia were delighted when their daughters asked them to pose for the cover of *Texas Twosomes*. As Donia Caspersen likes to say, "We're still married, but now our spouses live in heaven."

To my husband, Jimmy:
Thanks for believing
I love you

Doni

To Hil and the kids:
For being there
when I needed you

Colleen

Contents

Preface

The subject of a good marriage has always been fascinating to me. Growing up, I watched my parents meet the challenge of providing enough time and money for fourteen children, and still manage to keep their relationship intact. Throughout my marriage, I have held on to the premise that if they could do it, so could we. We did just fine through the first couple of decades.

Then we hit "the squeeze." For us that meant having three hormonally charged children who were basically sucking all the energy out of us. All we ever talked about was report cards, ball games, money, and work. Motivated by different interests, we found ourselves traveling down different roads at different times.

I started looking at couples who had a few more years of experience and were enjoying the relaxed portion of their journey. How did they get through their "squeeze" and stay friends? I wanted them to rewind their story, and show me how life looked when they were in our places.

How do people keep it together through babies, bankruptcy, demanding careers, accidents, illness, and all the other challenges that life thrusts upon us? If I needed to know, I figured so did others. I decided to write a book about marriages that have been through the fire and have the strength to show for it. These are people who still like each other after all the years. These are people who still choose each other over anybody else.

Texas Twosomes is a collection of stories about couples who have been married for twenty-five to seventy-five years. Sharing their hardships and lending advice, they sometimes enlighten and always entertain. Some of these names you'll recognize, others you won't—but famous or not, they all have stories worth reading.

Texas Twosomes is a celebration and an inspiration. Enjoy!

Acknowledgments

Endless thanks to God who smoothed our paths all the way to Eden, Mumford, Taylor and the other Texas towns where we found the "*Twosomes*."

And thanks to the twenty-five *Twosomes* who opened their hearts and shared their stories.

Finally, we appreciate our close family and friends who supported and encouraged us along the way.

–DCC & CDS

Senator Lloyd and B. A. (Longino) Bentsen

Wedding Date: November 27, 1943

You don't know anything about anybody when you marry them, so when you're blessed with a good marriage, it is truly a blessing. . . .
—B. A. Bentsen

For their first date, she thought they were going dancing, so she put on a velveteen dress and high heels. They ended up at the circus instead, where, B. A. recalls: "I tromped through all these muddy roads in silk shoes." Over the past fifty-five years, she's been willing to follow him anywhere. Happily, she says there hasn't been much mud on the journey. They celebrated their golden anniversary with a party at Washington's famous Blair House, courtesy of the president of the United States.

As much fun as it has been, political life has come with a high price. "A political career looks easy, I think, to a person who is sitting out front," says B. A. "But they don't know that you've done something four times before you see them and that you have five other places to go after you leave them. It makes for very long days."

She's not complaining. She wouldn't trade her years with Lloyd Bentsen for anything. "Marriage is absolutely the most miraculous thing in the world. You don't know anything about anybody when you marry them, so when you're blessed with a good marriage, it is truly a blessing. . . . Lloyd is a perfect husband. Doesn't that sound ridiculous? But he's wonderful, he really is."

You'll get no argument from him. He stepped down as secretary of the United States Treasury into a demanding law practice, where he continues to be consulted by the secretary of state. B. A. stays busy with

her children, grandchildren, and community work, but drops everything when her husband calls.

Tall, trim, and invariably well dressed, they always seem to have somewhere to go. Stealing an hour from his morning conference schedule, Lloyd and B. A. finally find time to look back over the years. From the twenty-sixth floor of a downtown Houston high-rise, surrounded by presidential pictures and plaques, they share their marriage story.

They first met in 1941 at The University of Texas in Austin. He was in law school, and she was working on a bachelor of science degree. After that date to the circus, they went out a few more times. But then he graduated from law school and signed up with the army.

When B. A. got her degree, she moved to New York where she became a fashion model with the Conover agency. With so much distance between them, their relationship took the slow track. That was fine with her since she was in no hurry to give her heart away: "I had been hurt as a young child. I had lost all my family and I was wary about relationships. I didn't want to go through that again."

By the time he figured out how much he cared about the brown-eyed beauty from East Texas, he was stationed in Brazil. The thunderbolt hit him when he ran into an old fraternity buddy who was headed back to the States on leave. Remembering that his friend had always had a thing for B. A., Lloyd got nervous.

He leans back in his chair and grins as he remembers what happened next. It was a race to get the girl.

> I said, "You're going back to New York, aren't you? I know damn well you are because that's where she is." I immediately went to the personnel officer and said, "I've got a crisis, I've got to get back to the States." When the officer asked if someone had died I said, "It's worse than that. A naval officer is about to marry an army officer's girlfriend."

Agreeing that this was an emergency situation, the officer informed Lloyd that the only way to get back to the States was to sign up for flight school.

"I've always wanted to fly," declared Lloyd. Then he called her in New York and told her, "Don't do anything foolish. I'll be right there."

Even after they set the date, there were still challenges to meet. On the morning of the wedding he called from the hospital where he was hemorrhaging from a tooth extraction. "Don't worry," he assured her. "I'll be there for the wedding tonight even if I have to go AWOL."

Wedding time came and he wasn't there. She remembers looking around that Baptist church in Columbia, Missouri, and taking a giant leap of faith. "I'm the only bride ever in this world who walked down the aisle without the groom standing there to greet her," B. A. recalls.

He finally arrived, but halfway through the ceremony he was hemorrhaging again. "I ran outside to the courtyard, grabbed a rock and pushed it into that cavity and came back in to marry the girl," says Lloyd.

With a mouth full of blood he mumbled, "I do?" This is one guy who really wanted to get married. "No," says the senator, gesturing toward the love of his life. "This is a guy who wanted to marry *her*."

After all these years, are there any regrets?

"Maybe one," he says with a sly smile. "I wish I had married her a year sooner."

> *Married couples who love each other*
> *tell each other a thousand things without talking.*
>
> –Chinese Proverb

Ben and Hedwig (Streit) Braun

Wedding Date: June 21, 1935

We just always go together.
—Ben Braun

It's a peaceful ride down the county road that leads to the house where Hedwig and Ben Braun have lived for almost thirty-five years. When you pull into the gravel driveway, Ben stands on the front porch, pointing out a place to park. With his steely blue eyes and sturdy build he lets me know that, despite being in his late eighties, he's still in charge around here. Then he leads me into the parlor to meet his bride.

"If there was anything like reincarnation, I'd hunt her up again," he says about the woman to whom he has been wed for more than six decades. Hedwig and Ben, with their German heritage, strict work ethic, and strong Christian faith, seem to be a match made in heaven. Ben points out that they've had their share of disagreements—the trick is to keep things from getting out of hand.

"We don't have any big fusses or anything like that," he says. "But when we don't agree and start arguing, one of us just shuts up and lets the other one have his way. It's best to shut up before you say something you'll regret." Hedwig nods her silver-haired head in agreement. "We never try to get the last word," she says.

They met in the spring of 1933 while Hedwig was a senior at Taylor High School. Members of the same Lutheran church, they didn't really meet until the day she hitched a ride with him to a swimming party. "He was in the front seat with his date and his brother was in the back seat with his date," she remembers. "I was the fifth wheel." The fact that she didn't have an escort was not a problem for the outgoing eighteen-year-old.

As soon as she got bored in the back seat, she climbed into the front seat to see what was going on up there. By the end of the ride, Ben was giving her more attention than his date. "He asked me to hold his watch while he went swimming. I conveniently forgot to give it back to him."

It was the beginning of something good. They went to hayrides and dances and hung out on the playground swinging their way into each other's hearts. Their feelings were growing, but they had no formal commitment, so Hedwig continued to accept invitations from other gentlemen. In the spring of 1935 she got his attention. "I came to see her one evening and she was out with somebody else," he recalls. "I said 'Whoa, this won't do.' I caught up with her that night and proposed to her."

He found her attractive, but it wasn't her good looks that made him pop the question. "I was raised as a Christian so that's what I was looking for, someone who I could respect for that. Mother and I talked about that a whole lot as I was growing up. A good person, somebody that would be a lasting attraction all my life."

They're both practical. When Hedwig's father offered them a choice between a big wedding and some bedroom furniture, they didn't hesitate for a moment. "I couldn't see and still can't see spending $8,000 or more on a dress that you're going to wear for thirty minutes," says Hedwig. "I bought a street dress that I could get some wear out of." The newlyweds toasted each other with fruit punch in her parents' home.

That sensible attitude carried them through the post-depression years and into 1944 when Ben joined the war effort. While serving his country in the Pacific from 1944-46, he sent home every paycheck. It was a tough time and, according to Ben, they couldn't save any money.

They continued to work hard. Ben was in the building business and Hedwig did administrative work. While providing for their family of six, they somehow managed to save for college and retirement. "I don't regret a thing," says Ben.

These days, they're still working. They love to bake and sometimes there are as many as 100 homemade cinnamon rolls in the freezer waiting for the next group of domino-playing buddies. She cooks, he does the dishes, and together they harvest the fruit from their garden. Opening a cabinet door, she shows off a shelf full of their latest effort. "We put up nine quarts of dill pickles just this morning."

Several years ago when Hedwig suffered a stroke and spent an extended stay in the hospital, he never left her side. Even after she regained her independence, he wouldn't go anywhere without her. "Where one goes, the other goes," Ben says. "We just always go together, it's automatic."

Marriage is three parts love and
seven parts forgiveness of sins.

–Langdon Mitchell

PROCARDIA

Dr. Dor and Virginia (Knight) Brown

Wedding Date: May 12, 1945

Of course there were times when we argued,
but we tried to straighten it out
before we went to bed.
—Virginia Brown

"He passed through town and I grabbed him," she says.

"That's not true. I grabbed you," he counters.

"What about all those beautiful women who were throwing themselves at your feet?" He winks and leans back in his chair. Sitting at the dining room table of their Fredericksburg home talking about old times, Dor and Virginia don't always agree on the details, but, in terms of the big picture, they do just fine.

They first got together in 1944. As a secretary in Norfolk, Virginia, at the time, she was determined to keep her distance from strangers in navy uniforms. That wasn't an easy feat in a town where the sailors outnumbered the civilians almost two to one. Even when the boss's daughter offered to fix her up with an attractive naval doctor, Virginia staunchly refused. "I do not date those 'fly by nights,'" she says. "I am going to marry a Virginia boy."

Later that night she and her date happened to run into the young doctor she had previously turned away. She says that as soon as she saw him at the officer's club her dislike for strangers in navy dress disappeared. At the end of the evening she went home and told her mother, "I have found the man I want to marry." She's still not sure what attracted her.

Dor knows. "It was my hair. I had a burr haircut and I charged her a quarter to feel my head."

They started seeing each other "every spare moment." About the time he was ready to propose, his overseas orders came through. "I remember it wasn't very romantic," Virginia recalls, her voice husky like Lauren Bacall's. "He said, 'you want to get married now or wait till I get back from Japan?'"

Eager as she was to marry him before he got shipped off, she insisted that they go to Texas first and meet his mom, dad, and sisters. An only child whose father had died when she was young, she knew the importance of family. More importantly, she didn't want to get off on the wrong foot with his older sisters, about whom she had already been warned. "They were convinced that the sun, moon, and stars were hung by Dor Brown," says Virginia.

He arrived in Texas a few days before she did, giving him plenty of time to concoct a story. "I told them Virginia was short and fat. When they asked what color her eyes were, I said, 'Which one?'"

By the time the Brown family piled into the car to pick Virginia up at the train station, the sisters didn't know what to think. Needless to say, they were relieved to see the pretty little brown-eyed brunette leave the train and walk toward them.

Bigger challenges came with the child-rearing years. According to Virginia, "The hardest part of marriage is raising children. Most of our disagreements have been over the boys. Of course, there were times when we argued but we tried to straighten it out before we went to bed.

"Actually, I got upset and he just looked at me. He got white around the lips and did a slow burn. We'd usually end up laughing. We tried not to argue in front of the children."

Dor is proud of the way they have hung together. "The children always knew that the two of us were first."

They've taken folk dancing, played couples' golf and bridge, and they enjoy regular outings to the horseraces, a testimony to the belief that a couple who plays together stays together. "I guess we are pretty compatible," says Virginia. "The golf pro said, in all his years of giving lessons, we're the only couple he's been able to teach *together*."

> *A good marriage is at least 80 percent good luck in finding the right person at the right time. The rest is trust.*
>
> –Nanette Newman (b. 1934), British actress

Dr. Exalton and Wilhelmina (Fitzgerald) Delco

Wedding Date: August 23, 1952

You do what you have to do
and you pray over the rest.
—WILHELMINA DELCO

"I'm the pushy one. My husband is the courtly, gentlemanly one. He steps back for all the ladies while I'm pushing to get to the front of the line."

That's Wilhelmina Fitzgerald Delco talking. The oldest of five, she was reared by a single mom in a housing project in Chicago. Exalton Delco grew up in Houston as a much-adored only child. They met at a small, historically black college in Nashville, Tennessee—Fisk University. Both are well-educated, family-oriented, and community-minded, but that's where the similarities end.

Having spent many years as a college dean, he originated the law of the "Five P's"—Prior preparation prevents poor performance. "He prepares everything in detail way ahead of time," she says. "My motto is don't do today what you can put off till tomorrow because tomorrow you might not have to do it." She cracks up at her self-evaluation. Her laughter is infectious. "People just don't understand why we can get along. I talk and he does."

It's easy to see why she was so effective in state politics; she gets fired up just talking about her favorite topics—children and education. As the first black elected to public office in Travis County, she has always felt called to do her part. "My husband teases me about having a built-in radar for all non-paying jobs. But I've always felt passionately about trying to increase the quality of life for children."

He sits in his overstuffed chair and watches her like a movie he's seen before but still isn't sure how it turns out. "I think I get very exasperating to him," she says, slipping off her shoes and settling into the couch cushions. "Sometimes it seems the harder I push the slower he goes."

Does she drive him crazy? "Occasionally," he says, choosing his words carefully. "She refuses to stay in a room near the elevator or that has a bad view. When we go to a hotel there is always a series of room changes." After all these years, he has learned not to unpack his suitcase until she has scoped things out. She shakes her head while he talks. "If I wanted a room that looked out on the parking lot, why would I come to Denver? I want to see the mountains. I want to open the drapes and look out onto the horizon. Exalton says a hotel room is the place where you sleep."

They've laughed and they've cried together. The hardest time was in the early '70s when Exalton suffered a devastating automobile accident which left him in a body cast for eighteen months. At one point, the doctors thought he might lose both an eye and a leg. Wilhelmina was determined that he get through it in one piece. “It never occurred to me that he might not recover. My job was to keep a quality of life and an air of optimism for him. You do what you have to do and pray over the rest.”

She set up his hospital bed in the family room where he wouldn’t be isolated and pureed three meals a day for him until his jaw healed. He remembers it as a time of frustration because all he could do was look around and see what needed to be done. “It was a period during which I saw things coming apart but I also remember the immense support and empathy I got from my wife.”

She focuses on the good that came out of it. “The word spread in Austin that my husband had had an accident and we experienced the most incredible outpouring of support that you could imagine.”

His recovery was hard, but it brought them closer. “He’s my best friend. Absolutely. After I’ve smiled at everybody else all day, I can come home and tell him the truth. He’s just my best friend.”

He says they’ve never been into keeping secrets. “I don’t have to hold back on how I feel. We lay out the facts. On the basis of what the facts show, then we’ll decide what to do. There is always some give and take in there.”

Exalton thinks most couples get married before they really know what they are getting into. “I think a number of folk have not seen their prospective spouse without the glitter and glamour of make-up and all that. I think people need to see each other in a natural light. We courted for five years. That’s one thing that helped us.”

Two is not twice one.
Two is a thousand times one.

–G. K. Chesterton

Roy and Tootsie (Balagia) Guerrero

Wedding Date: February 28, 1943

There's strength in diversity.
—Roy Guerrero

When Roy Guerrero started hanging out with the Balagia girls, he had no idea he would end up marrying one of them. He just knew there was plenty of fun to be had at their house. "It was Grand Central Station," he recollects. "And I've always liked to be where the action is."

Sitting in the living room of their white frame house where they reared their five children, they seem a bit shy about sharing their story. Roy admits that he still feels a bit guilty about taking Tootsie away from her family when she was so young. She was fifteen and he was twenty-one when they first met.

It all started when Roy and his buddies began stopping by the house on their way to dances at The University of Texas to invite the Balagia girls and friends to come along with them. One of the other girls usually beat Tootsie to the seat next to Roy, but she didn't mind. They were just a bunch of kids out for a good time.

At some point, and neither Roy nor Tootsie remembers exactly when it happened, they started doing a little slow dancing. She suddenly knew she was in love with the stocky young man with the kind eyes. "It was when a friend of mine started showing interest in Roy. That's when I realized I didn't want her to have him. I wanted him for myself."

Tootsie's parents were leery. They were Catholic, Lebanese, and upper middle class, while the Guerreros were Protestant, Hispanic, and barely getting by on the income Roy's father earned as a minister. In spite of her parents' feelings, she and Roy were ready to cross

cultural, religious, and economic boundaries to be together. "There's strength in diversity," Roy says.

Unconvinced, Tootsie's dad did everything he could to break them up, including trying to marry her off to more suitable partners. Right after her eighteenth birthday, he sent her to stay with relatives in Houston. A few days later Roy jumped in his car and raced down I-10 heading east. He walked right into Aunt Margaret's house and smooth-talked her into letting Tootsie go out for lunch, promising he'd bring her right back. Two hours later she was back at her auntie's home and he was back on the highway.

By the time Tootsie returned to her parents in Austin, they had had a change of heart. Finally accepting the fact that the youngsters were in love, they started planning an elaborate engagement party. On a Saturday night in the spring of 1943, Tootsie and Roy found themselves surrounded by cake, candles, and flowers. Then, in the midst of all the champagne toasts and well wishing, they made an announcement that blew the crowd off their feet. They were already married.

The lunch date that began at Aunt Margaret's had ended with a trip to the First Presbyterian Church, where Roy and Tootsie promised to love and obey until death did them part. Needless to say, Roy's relationship with his new in-laws was a bit tense after they heard the news. He apologized and apologized and finally, after sending them a mariachi band serenade, he won the Balagias' blessing.

As it turned out, their cultural differences didn't pose as much of a challenge as the fact that Tootsie and Roy come from opposite ends of the personality profile. "Roy wakes up every day with a smile and says, 'Good morning, Lord!'" Tootsie says. "I wake up and gasp, 'Good Lord, it's morning!'"

Whatever the reason, the first years were tough. "I was used to everything being done for me," says Tootsie. "My room was cleaned, my laundry was done for me. I didn't know whether an egg was supposed to be baked or boiled."

She needn't have worried. In between working and finishing his degree at The University of Texas, Roy took the time to teach his bride anything she needed in the way of domestic skills. According to Tootsie, Roy knew how to do everything. "He was amazing," she says.

She also learned her way around the kitchen. Before long she was making the chicken enchiladas that he loved, as well as the kibbe and grape leaves that her mother had served. She was merging their worlds with her culinary skills, and with all those kids and a hungry husband, it was a good idea.

Roy admits that having a bigger bank account might have made life easier, but he wouldn't trade Tootsie staying at home with the kids or his extended career with the parks department for anything in the world. "It was a decision we were happy with but you don't get rich serving the city," he explains.

After more than five decades, life has come full circle. Now, it is their house that looks like Grand Central Station with kids, grandkids, friends, and neighbors dropping by constantly. Tootsie loves it. "If there is nothing on the stove when my kids come over they say, 'Are you sick Mama?'"

Retired, Roy stays busy with family and community projects, but Tootsie will always be his priority. "I still bring her flowers," he says. "We walk in different directions but we manage to keep holding hands."

The man who finds a wife finds a good thing.
She is a blessing to him from the Lord.

–Proverbs 18:22

Tony and Mercy (Trevino) Hinojosa

Wedding Date: February 10, 1962

If you're not married . . .
your life doesn't bloom out.
—Tony Hinojosa

Tony and Mercy Hinojosa are sitting in their Houston house near Hobby Airport watching two of their grandchildren chase each other around the living room. When I tell them they don't look old enough to have grandchildren they look at each other and grin. They've heard that line before. They were so young when they got married they had to have their parents' permission. "We had to take our daddies along to the courthouse with us," laughs Mercy.

"We were too young to know that we were too young," adds Tony. Mercy says that when she proposed marriage, it was more of a statement than a request. "I told him he had to marry me and he said 'okay.'"

Her parents, however, didn't think it was okay, and they tried to talk the youngsters out of it. But being in love with a baby on the way, Tony and Mercy were determined. They traded vows on February 10, 1962, on her seventeenth birthday. He was twenty.

They moved into the garage apartment behind Tony's parents' house where his parents and eight brothers and sisters lived. They had some privacy, but luxuries were few and far between. "I remember we'd cash a check for $10 on Wednesday and it had to last till Friday," she says. "Money was tight."

Then one day while Tony was parking cars at a country club, a local caterer approached him about tending bar at an upcoming party. "I didn't know beans about mixing drinks," he says, but he jumped at the chance to make more money. It turned out he was a natural in the party business and pretty soon Mercy was working right along with him.

They quickly became favorites with Houston's upper crust. "People were always saying, 'Oh we want that little Hispanic couple,'" Mercy says. Ten years later they had their own business.

Although Tony has never given up his work as a machinist, he helps Mercy cater whenever he can and he's convinced that sharing a business has enhanced their relationship. "I think working parties has kind of grown us together. We work real good together."

When their five sons were small he worked all the time and Mercy did most of the childrearing alone. "For the first ten years it was hard. I had to deal with the kids by myself. We used to fight about that. I always said, 'You need to spend time with the boys.'"

Tony must have done something right, because, now that they're grown, his sons come visiting every chance they get. Tony and Mercy's work schedules still leave little time for leisure, so they have a routine that keeps them in touch. "Our private time is ten o'clock in the morning until noon.

We go on errands together and we go to lunch. We visit real good. I always ask her 'How was your day?'"

Mercy believes that being firstborn children from big families helped them learn what it takes to get along. "We don't hardly ever get mad any more. We used to fight about money. But that was only because we didn't have enough of it," she says and then she grins. "Basically, I do what I need to do and he doesn't ever question it. He's easy to live with. He goes along."

"It's called manipulation," he jokes. The only time he really gets angry is when people manipulate his wife. "I get mad because I see a lot of her friends take advantage of her. I say, 'Mercy, what's wrong with you? You can't let them do you like that.'"

"I think people should go with the flow," she responds. "If things happen that you can change, do it. Otherwise, go with the flow." The fact is their contrasting personalities seem to balance each other out. "He is laid back, I'm real hyper," she said. "Tony loves TV and I say *let's go, we gotta go*."

"She always takes on too many jobs," he says shaking his head. "This is a time when all the kids are gone and we should be slowing down a little. Instead, we're busier and busier. Every year goes by faster."

One thing for sure, she's never going to change. "Her work is her fuel. I'm just starting to understand that." As Tony makes room in his easy chair for a wiggly two-year-old, he thinks about what attracted him to Mercy in the first place. "My favorite thing is her warmth. And her laughter."

Sometimes Tony threatens to get his own apartment so he can finally get some peace and quiet. The truth is he'd dearly miss the chaos. "I'm glad I got married young. I still feel like a thirty-year-old. I recommend marriage. If you're not married, your life doesn't grow. It doesn't bloom out."

> *A wise woman always lets her husband have her way.*
>
> –R. B. Sheridan (1751–1815)

Jim and Kathy (Caspersen) Jamail

Wedding Date: July 31, 1971

The way we got through it was
patience and prayer.
–KATHY JAMAIL

It was Christmas Eve 1968 and Jimmy Jamail was looking for a date. He was back home after a two-year stint in the army and his little black book wasn't exactly bulging with the names of eligible females. Luckily, his buddy Cas offered assistance. "Come home with me," he said. "I got ten sisters. One of 'em is bound to be free."

So Jimmy went to Cas' house and turned on the charm. "I came through the front door and yelled, 'Anybody want to go to a party?' Kathy was sitting in the next room all dressed up for midnight mass. Without a moment's hesitation she called out, 'I do.'"

Sitting around the kitchen table of their Houston home, they're taking a walk down memory lane. Kathy said their first date was not exactly the stuff of romance novels. "He was okay but I was dating lots of other people," she recalls. "I was enjoying a newfound popularity and I wasn't about to date just one person."

But that didn't mean that he liked sharing: "I showed up at her apartment once when we were s'posed to go somewhere and she came in about an hour later. She gave me some lame excuse about how the guy wouldn't bring her home."

Sometime during that first year, Jimmy started falling in love. "I remember exactly where we were when I first said 'I love you.' I couldn't even believe that I had said it. I didn't want to, but I couldn't help myself."

It took Kathy by surprise as well. "It scared me. It meant he was serious and I wasn't ready for serious." They continued to

go out and at some point during the winter of 1971 her heart caught up with his. The next thing they knew, she was flashing an engagement ring. Every one of their siblings (she's the oldest of fourteen, he's the oldest of seven) was in their July wedding—a big formal ceremony at the Catholic church Kathy had been attending since her childhood. The lively reception was marked by a steady stream of champagne toasts and Lebanese dancing.

After the honeymoon, Jimmy came back to the family grocery business, in which he had been working since he was a little kid. Kathy went back to teaching second graders. Both from big families, they were ecstatic over every one of the six babies they brought home from the hospital. But as their number of offspring grew, their "couple time" shrank. They started a tradition of getting away from it all for one night every few months. Since business didn't allow much vacation time, instead of traveling to another city they simply drove to the closest luxury hotel. "We'd order movies and dinner," Kathy says. "We'd stay up late, then take naps and read. We did exactly what we wanted. We were like kids in a candy store."

Mainly they focused on each other. "We crammed a lot into that twenty-four-hour period and we never left the room," says Jimmy with a smile. "We were definitely not interested in what was going on downstairs."

In spite of the fact that they nurtured the relationship, circumstances took their toll. The family store underwent a change of ownership and forced Jimmy out. As he agonized over what to do next, their twelve-year-old son, Chuck, developed leukemia. He died two days after the doctors made their diagnosis. In less than a year, their world had fallen apart.

The following year they opened their own grocery store but the losses of the previous months took their toll. "We lost our son, our business. I was building a new store, Kathy was real involved in volunteer work," he remembers. "We lost each other for awhile."

The future looked grim. "There were many days when we didn't even want to be around each other," says Kathy. "The way we got through it was patience and prayer. We had to do a lot of waiting." She credits her therapist for encouraging her to reach out to Jimmy in spite of the way she felt about him. "I remember the day I walked by him in the kitchen and touched his shoulder as I passed. It was a turning point."

They started spending his afternoon off together and, little by little, they rediscovered their attraction for each other. They found out you can't put your married life on autopilot no matter how many years you have under your marital belt. "You have to work at marriage all the time," he says. "When you're young, everything's easy. There's a lot of physical attraction, a lot of passion. When you get older, things get in the way."

"We hung on to the commitment," she says, leaning into him. "Some days it was all we had."

> *A successful marriage is an edifice that must be rebuilt every day.*
>
> –André Maurois (1885-1967) French writer

Speaker of the House
Pete and Nelda (McQuien) Laney

Wedding Date: August 10, 1963

I think a lot of couples . . . get married with this big plan in life instead of just rolling with the punches.
—Nelda Laney

I met the Laneys at the state capitol. As Speaker of the Texas House of Representatives, Pete leads our legislative body toward responsible lawmaking, while she makes sure the capitol stays family friendly. A positive, outgoing individual, Nelda loves her work. "I enjoy being the unofficial 'Mom' of the Capitol," she says. Last year the legislature passed a resolution naming her "First Lady of the Texas House."

Flinching at the word politics, they prefer to think of their work as taking care of people. "It's something we can do to help," she explains. Walking the marbled floors of the rotunda, they shake hands with virtually everyone they pass. They seem to be on a first-name basis with everybody in the place.

A self-described "country boy," Pete grew up in Hale Center, where his grandfather came to farm cotton in 1905. Nelda was born in Post and grew up in Plainview. They met each other in Lubbock during their freshman year at Texas Tech. "We never really were introduced," he recalls. "I was at a basketball game one night and she walked in with someone I knew." He thought she was attractive, so he bet his roommate ten dollars he could get a date with her. "I found out later that she only went with me to make her boyfriend jealous. It was a quid pro quo deal," he grinned. "But that didn't matter to me. Ten bucks is ten bucks."

Nelda thinks she may have caught his eye when she walked across the stage at the Hale Center Fourth of July "Miss Firecracker" contest the summer before. "I was lucky enough to win the contest and the lady who made my crown was Pete's grandmother."

It appears they were meant to be. "We came from the same values," Pete says. "That made it very easy to communicate." When they got married at the end of their sophomore year, she changed her major to education so she could teach school in Hale Center while Pete ran the family farm. It was a plan that changed a bit when he got the opportunity to run for state legislator.

Being flexible has taken them far. "I think a lot of couples, or at least some who break up, get married with this big plan in life instead of just rolling with the punches," says Nelda. "I'd never dreamed that we'd be in the public eye. Did you Pete? No, you didn't. I thought we were going to live out in the country and farm for the rest of our lives.

"You go off to college and intend to marry someone from far off and live in a big house on a tree-lined street. After we had that date on that Friday night, we didn't either one ever date anyone else."

This same woman who travels around Texas giving speeches and doing press conferences on behalf of the Speaker of the House doesn't mind getting up from the dinner table to get her husband a glass of milk. It drives her daughters crazy but Nelda likes waiting on her husband.

Still, she can't resist an occasional dig over the way he drops his clothes on the floor and eats too many chicken fried steaks. It's clear that looking after him is a job she enjoys. Even now, after all their years of togetherness, she's still very impressed with the man she married. "Even though I've lived with it, you know, I am still amazed at his character. He keeps so cool in the fire. He truly has a *try to get along and work out the problems* kind of personality."

Although they are an outgoing couple, they keep their deepest emotions to themselves. When their third child died, they found comfort only in each other. "We were there for each other," Nelda confides. "We didn't say a whole lot but we really leaned on each other. For us, it made it easier not to dwell on it."

Do they have any problems? "As far as big marriage problems, no," says Nelda. "We haven't really had those. We've been really lucky." They do have one bad habit, he says. "We take each other for granted a lot."

"A lot," she agrees. "Continually. I mean, look, he's got a maid . . . somebody who picks up after him all the time. What does he have to gripe about?"

He actually admits to being a burden. "I'm a load," he says and looks over at Nelda.

She shrugs her shoulders. "I guess we do agree on everything."

Marriage is one long conversation,
checquered by disputes.

–Robert Louis Stevenson (1850-1894)

Philip and Bobbie (Maddox) Lockett

Wedding Date: August 14, 1954

We're best friends. That's it in a nutshell.
—Bobbie Lockett

He used to spend the night with her older brother. His grandmother went to her granny's house for tea. Having grown up in the same small West Texas town, Philip and Bobbie Maddox Lockett can barely remember a time when their paths didn't cross. "We've grown up together," Bobbie says. He smiles: "The only time I think we may have too much togetherness is when people call her Phillis and me Bob."

Watching them on the couch finishing each other's sentences and laughing at each other's jokes, it's easy to see they don't mind the occasional confusion. Over the past forty-five years, they've reared children, managed ranches, worked at the church, and stayed best friends every step of the way.

Having known Philip most of her life, she didn't feel the tug on her heartstrings until her sophomore year in high school. It happened when he came back from a rehab center where he had been recuperating from polio. Maybe it was the walking stick that caught her eye. "I think one of the reasons I was so attracted to him was because he had that cane. It was kind of debonair or something."

Philip throws his head back and laughs. He's never heard that one before. It was probably her baby blues that did it for him: "I can't hardly narrow it down, but I've always been a person who noticed eyes. She has such pretty eyes."

They wanted a big church wedding after high school graduation but a drought took its toll on the family finances and, instead, they made the short trip to Venus, Texas, where Philip's

brother, a Methodist minister, pronounced them man and wife. She wore a blue polished cotton ankle-length dress with satin shoes, and Philip wore his first new suit.

They've always been ranchers except for a time when he served on the San Angelo police force. Even when he worked seven days a week, they made time for each other on his afternoons off. "We'd go out to eat or to a movie or even work in the yard together," Bobbie recalls. According to Philip, certain phases of parenting were more challenging than others, especially the teenage years. "When their mother told them something, I was with her. I'd say 'Now that's the way it's gonna be, kids. Don't try to get me to change.' We always stuck together."

It has not always been easy. Philip's life long struggle with asthma has really put them through their paces. Bobbie remembers one night when she was particularly fearful: "He woke up at 1:00 A.M. with an attack and our doctor had to drive out—we lived six miles out in the country—in the middle of the night and give Philip several shots . . . We had many anxious moments."

Through it all, they have tried not to take themselves too seriously. One time, in an attempt to qualify for a government program, they decided to sow grass seed on ninety-five acres. Bobbie drove while Philip sat in the bed of the truck monitoring the machine that threw out the seeds. This incident was a memorable one for Philip:

> Pretty soon I got to hollering 'cause I thought she wasn't driving in the right place. She didn't say anything at first and then she suddenly hit the brakes and I found myself practically standing on my head behind the cab. Then she stuck her head out the window and said in a real sweet voice, "What did you say, honey?"

It was the first and last time he ever tried to tell her what to do.

She puts her hand on his shoulder and says, "Philip was a woman's libber before it was fashionable. Not in the militant sense but in the sense that he has always known that women are as smart and capable as men."

A while back, they sold their ranch and moved to town to live in a house that belonged to his mother and father. They painted, tiled, and hammered for months, making it just the way they wanted it. Always in the middle of some project, they seem to be happiest when working together. Bobbie sums it up this way: "We're best friends. That's it in a nutshell."

The plural of spouse is spice.

–Christopher Morley (1890-1957), American novelist

Dr. John and Helen "Pinky" (Smith) McKetta

Wedding Date: October 17, 1943

If we had tried to use a computer to match us, it would have gone up in smoke.
—John McKetta

It's 7:00 A.M. on a Monday and Pinky and John McKetta are sitting at the kitchen table playing cribbage and drinking coffee. Ready for the office, John wouldn't think about leaving before his daily card game with Pinky. They take their play very seriously. Keeping things fun has helped them get along for the past five and a half decades. For those of us who aspire to such a relationship, they recommend holding hands in public and kissing hello and goodbye.

In his mid-twenties, John was doing graduate work in engineering at the University of Michigan when he walked into the administration office one day and made the acquaintance of young Helen Smith. "I started asking her to marry me three weeks after we met," he says. "She just fit perfectly into the pattern of what I wanted."

Her intention had been to stay single and join the women's division of the armed services. Somehow, her date with Uncle Sam seemed less pressing after meeting the brash and funny graduate student named Johnny

McKetta. In keeping with his outgoing personality, he nicknamed her Pinky on their first date. By the sound of his surname, she thought she'd found a fellow Scotchman until he told her that his father had emigrated from the Ukraine. "It was the second greatest disappointment when she found out I wasn't Scotch-Irish," he says with a wink. "I'm not allowed to tell the biggest disappointment."

They got married in Ann Arbor on his birthday, then took a boat to Cleveland and, due to a shortage of cash, hitchhiked to Uniontown, Pennsylvania. They spent their honeymoon at

his sister's house. "When we got married, Pinky had seventy dollars and I had five dollars. Ever since that time whenever we got some money it was always split 14-1 in Pinky's favor."

After earning his Ph.D., John was hired as an assistant professor in the Chemical Engineering Department of The University of Texas in Austin and with her support, he climbed the academic ladder to the top. Dividing her time between the kids and the community, Pinky's never felt any conflict about having a career outside the home. It's been a jam-packed journey. "Johnny has a lot of passion," she says of him. "Life with him is a three-ring circus."

Early on, she developed a practice of slipping notes of encouragement under the glass on his desk. *Big shots were once little shots that just kept on shooting*, says one. *When we're wrong, let's be willing to change and when we're right, let's be easy to live with*, says another. If he ever needs a dose of humility, she is ready with that too. He says that comes in handy for a college professor. He has saved every note she's ever written.

Crazy about all four of their children, they consider their daughter Mary Anne a special blessing. Because of her need for round the clock care, she's lived at the Austin State School since she was six. They look forward to being with her every week, letting nothing interfere with their Saturday morning visits. "I think we're lucky," says Pinky. "We have three sons. And then we have this fourth child, Mary Anne, who is a great benefit to the family. I think she has been a character builder for the boys."

He's an engineer; she loves literature. He likes prize fighting; she prefers the arts. "If we had tried to use a computer to match us it would have gone up in smoke," he confesses. But they do have a lot in common—they both love to play cards, shoot pool, travel, and give "graduate picnics" on the lawn of their lakeside home. "We're also great at a crossword puzzle," says Pinky. "He can do some of it, I can do some of it, together we can complete the whole thing."

By all means marry; if you get a good wife you'll become happy; if you get a bad one, you'll become a philosopher.

–Socrates (469-399 B.C.)

Dr. Luka and Lela (Pecanic) Milas

Wedding Date: November 3, 1962

Harmonize, just harmonize.
–LUKA MILAS

It's a rainy Wednesday afternoon and Luka and Lela Milas are taking a break from their normal routine. As head of cancer research at one of M.D. Anderson's research laboratories, he is often up to his ears in laboratory work at this time of day. She's usually showing houses to a client.

Today they are sitting across from each other in their living room, discussing the ups and downs of the last thirty-six years. He teases her. She shoves him playfully. "My husband," she says in an accent reminiscent of Zsa Zsa Gabor, "I love him more every day."

Things are good. All three of their children are grown, their dreams are within reach, and they have settled into the cozy West University lifestyle they've been working toward their whole life. It hasn't always been this comfortable.

Growing up behind communist lines, survival was the name of the game for both of them. Luka's older brother was killed for his political beliefs, and Lela watched Party officials force their way onto their Croatian farm and confiscate portions of the family harvest. "We watched and grew with Communism," says Lela. "I still have it in front of my eyes."

Education was clearly the way out. They met at the University of Zagreb in 1960, where Luka was studying medicine and Lela was finishing up a degree in linguistics. On long walks across campus, they shared stories from the past and dreams for the future. Luka says he was a goner even before he found out how smart she was. He recalls: "I didn't know her, but I saw she was beautiful."

"We instantly loved each other," she says. Two years later, they said "I do."

But it didn't happen the way she had imagined. "I just couldn't ask my parents to spend extra money for a white dress even though it was one of my dreams as a human female being. Instead, I got married in a two-piece suit that I could continue wearing for the next five years."

The ceremony took place in a Catholic church in Croatia, and afterward they sat down to a home-cooked meal of *pecena pura* (roasted turkey) and *sarma* (saurkraut-stuffed cabbage rolls) with about a hundred loved ones at her parents' house. Family blessings were dished out along with the main course.

The newlyweds soon moved to Houston where Luka finished his post-doctoral work at M.D. Anderson. Over the next several years, they went back and forth from America to their homeland. In spite of the gratifying work he was doing in the States, he longed for home. "I had always dreamed of helping my own people in my own country," he explains.

That was not to be. As Luka puts it, "The only people who could succeed in my old country would be those who were Party members. That communist system pushed you out in one way or another."

Caring for three children on a researcher's salary was difficult says Lela, "Sometimes we could barely put two ends together." As he watches the sun coming out from behind a cloud, Luka says he doesn't remember hard times. "If you really want to know, I don't believe we have had hardships in our thirty-six years," he says. "We have a strong desire to achieve in this world as a family, she and I. We put all our energy together for that. She is a person for home, for family . . . incredible."

Lela has had her *orehnjaca* (cake) and eaten it too. She stayed home with her children when they were young, entered the teaching profession when they hit school age, and has spent the past several years selling residential real estate. Family comes first, but they also love their work. They want to advertise the fact that a good marriage comes with strong commitment. For Lela, marriage boils down to this:

> I'd like to use a big microphone all over the U.S. and Croatia to tell this. When difficulty comes, you cannot give up, you cannot become impatient. Love is love. It may change from time to time but it goes hand in hand with respect. That makes strong healthy base for life together, for marriage. When the deep waters of the ocean are calm, small waves on the surface do not make storm.

Luka is inspired by the words of his *Otac* ("daddy"). "I have never forgotten what my father said when we first got married: "Harmonize, just harmonize."

> *The whole art of marriage lies in the ability*
> *to pass from love to friendship without sacrificing love.*
> –André Maurois (1885-1967) French writer

Cornelius "Neal" and Natalie (Dufner) Phelan

Wedding Date: April 26, 1944

Number one, a couple has got to enjoy being with each other.
—Neal Phelan

In 1943 Neal Phelan was twenty-eight years old and working at a flying school in Cuero, Texas. He and the other instructors spent their days teaching young men to fly and their evenings flirting with the waitresses in the mess hall. One day, a pretty young girl from nearby Halletsville joined the cafeteria wait staff. Ten years younger than he and naive as a child, she reminded him of his five younger sisters in Beaumont whom he missed terribly. Today he claims, "At first I kind of treated her like another baby sister."

That included giving her advice on how to get along with her boyfriend. One day she came to work with a broken heart and he became a regular "Dear Abby." Halfway through the counseling session he came to his senses: "All of a sudden I started to tell her something and I thought, *You crazy damn fool. That's the gal you been lookin' for your whole life*."

He told her how he felt, she gave her boyfriend the boot, and they started going out dancing and bowling every week. They also talked on the phone every day. When her parents moved to a place in the country that didn't have a phone, he started sending her letters.

But he didn't depend on the United States Postal Service. At the end of his daily flying lessons he would instruct his student pilot to fly low enough so he could toss his messages out of the cockpit over her house. A few of them landed on the roof and others got lost in the fields but she was able to find most of them. A couple of them actually ended up on the front porch. She still has one. It's torn and yellow but you can tell by the way she smooths the edges when she holds on to it, it means a

lot to her. These days, Natalie smiles a lot but she doesn't say much. In 1982 she suffered a stroke that greatly diminished her walking and talking skills. She uses a wheelchair to get around but mostly she depends on Neal. The miracle is that neither one of them is complaining. "We have been closer since her surgery than we were the first thirty-five years," says Neal. "We need each other so much more now. If I didn't have her, I'd be lost. I wouldn't know what to do."

"She's still the boss," he says, cocking his head in her direction. "Don't let anybody tell you any different."

Digging through a box of old pictures, he finds a photograph of them in the coffee shop where he gave her the engagement ring. He handed it to her over a plate of liver and onions. They married at the Catholic church in Cuero with family members looking on. He was decked out in his flight commander uniform, and she wore a cream-colored suit and high heels. He stood on his tiptoes for the pictures.

Natalie grew up around horses, so Neal took her to a dude ranch in Bandera for their honeymoon. She had a wonderful time, but he required medical treatment after the first day. "I had blisters on my hiney," he remembers. "That riding liked to kill me."

When they got home they discovered another bump in the road. Neither of them knew how to cook. Describing their first meal, he laughs so hard he almost falls out of his chair. She laughs, too. "We stuck a roast in a skillet. Whenever it got brown on one side, we'd turn it. Then we just cut off the cooked part and ate it."

There was no plan for how many kids they would have but Natalie gave birth on a regular and frequent schedule until the house was filled with five sons and three daughters. She managed the children during the day but they knew who was in charge when he came home. A rowdy bunch, the Phelan kids were on a first-name basis with the staff of the hospital emergency room.

When it came time for the kids to go to college, Neal started looking for a way to enhance his income. He talked to Natalie about the possibility of buying a hearing aid company. It meant using every bit of their savings to buy a business they knew nothing about. "She said, 'If that's what you want, let's do it.' Natalie has always been the kind of person who could work things out," he says.

Neal believes a good relationship hinges on two things: "Number one, a couple has got to enjoy being with each other. They must also have a need for each other. She fills up the things I'm short of, that I need help with, and vice versa. I respect her and she respects me." Then he grins that crinkly-eyed grin. "And she hardly ever hits me with anything heavier than a broom."

One of the best hearing aids a man can have
is an attentive wife.

–Groucho Marx

Rev. Herman Island and Daisy (Scott) Phillips

Wedding Date: August 25, 1949

If you marry me, I'll see to it that you love me.
—Rev. Phillips

Love at first sight. That's how Rev. Herman Island Phillips describes his first encounter with Daisy Scott at a college in East Texas. He was a student and she was a teacher. The first time he walked into class and laid eyes on the beautiful, young English professor, he started hearing wedding bells. Unfortunately, she didn't hear a thing.

"I wasn't looking for anybody," says Daisy. "My goal was to get a Ph.D in English and buy my momma a home." And that's exactly what she told the love-struck student when he asked her to marry him one day after class. "You have all the qualities that I like in a man," she told him, "I just don't happen to love you." Undaunted, the aspiring young preacher replied, "If you marry me, I'll see to it that you love me."

The Reverend says, "the Lord had put her in my heart," and he wasn't about to ignore a message of that magnitude. So he started writing her letters every day. If those love notes didn't win her over, at least they got her attention. She corrected the grammar and handed them right back to him. He throws his head back and laughs at the memory. "She marked that red pencil all over them!"

She finally started taking him seriously one weekend when he gave her a ride to Houston to visit her mother. According to him, the courtship was under way before they made it to the highway. "I got her out of that professional climate," he says. "That's when I got to know her pretty good."

He may have been moving down the road with Daisy, but he still had a long way to go with her mother, who was counting on

her youngest daughter to take care of her in her twilight years. Mrs. Scott was so opposed to their marriage she refused to help sew the bridesmaids' dresses even though she was a professional seamstress.

That hurt plenty. But as painful as it was back then, Daisy now sees her mother's resistance as a positive thing. "Momma got everybody all stirred up against us. The more the relatives fussed, the more I dug my heels in. Reverend and I grew closer together and we've been that way ever since."

It was hard for the Reverend too, but he never let his mother-in-law's attitude get to him. In fact, he was so determined to win her over he invited her to come along on the honeymoon. To this day, he says it's one of the smartest things he ever did. "Whatever I bought for Daisy, I'd buy for my mother-in-law. By the end of the trip, she loved me."

Over the years, Daisy and the Reverend have spent their time preaching, teaching, rearing five sons, and running their own lawnmowing service. As soon as they could walk, the boys started going with their dad to cut grass. Sometimes, when she wasn't busy in the classroom, Daisy went along too. "We'd carry a big old jug of lemonade with us and have a picnic every day," she says.

These days she leaves the lawns to him but supports his church ministry by cooking for his congregation every weekend. They tote lunch to Fort Worth every Sunday morning where he delivers a sermon at the Morning Star Baptist Church. The weekly commute may sound tedious, but to this couple, whose work kept them apart during the first years of their marriage (while she taught in Crockett, he pastored in Palestine; his church was in Brownwood when her school was in Houston), that weekly drive is an adventure. "We got a little place where we stop and get coffee," Daisy tells me. "Mostly, we talk and laugh. That's how we handle anything that we can't do something about. We laugh it to death."

Humor helps, but the real secret lies in knowing how to hang in there. Having buried three sons, they know about suffering. "Jesus Christ is the captain of our salvation and he was made perfect through suffering," says the Reverend in a voice he usually saves for the pulpit. "We're supposed to suffer, too. Perfection only comes through suffering."

Daisy's advice is more earthy. "Just be one fool at a time," she says.

Something happened one day after they'd been married about twenty years that really helped the Reverend put things in perspective. It was a Saturday morning and he was out mowing their eleven-acre tract when a piece of wire got caught in the motor of the tractor. He shoved the vehicle into neutral and then crawled underneath to check out the problem. About that same time Daisy looked out the kitchen window to check on him. Seeing him on his back under the tractor, she let her imagination get the better of her.

Flying out the back door, she climbed a barbed wire fence and was so relieved to find him okay that she covered his face with kisses and tears. It was a moment he'll never forget. "Every once in a while you need something to stir things up a little," he smiles, showing off his deep dimples. "After that happened I said, *This woman really loves me*."

Therefore shall a man leave his father and his mother and shall cleave unto his wife and they shall be one flesh.

—Genesis 2:24

Chevron
Jim

Edward "Jim" and Mary (Como) Randall

Wedding Date: March 20, 1965

I know the only reason you're staying with me
is cuz the Lord told you to.
–Jim Randall

When Jim Randall and Mary Como exchanged their vows at the Little Zion Baptist Church in Beaumont, they had no idea how fiercely those promises would be tested. More than thirty years later, they can say they have been through the fire.

It's about 9:00 A.M. on a Friday and Jim has just come through the back door with a bag full of fresh fruit and cinnamon rolls. Having checked on his workers at the job site, he has stopped by the grocery store for Mary's breakfast. He has always enjoyed taking care of his wife.

They met in the summer of 1963 at his uncle's house in Beaumont when he was nineteen and she was seventeen. She had lived in Beaumont all her life and he had just moved there from Louisiana for a job with his uncle's construction company. As soon as the introductions were made, he asked her to go for a ride in his brother's car. Directing him all over town, she had him picking up her girlfriends along the way. "We had a ball," she remembers. "He was going everywhere I'd point."

It was more than just fun for him and he told her so when he took her home that afternoon. "I'm going to be as nice to you as I possibly can because I'm going to marry you," he said. She was shocked. They had known each other for a total of three hours. "I thought this guy is crazy," she recalls. "I couldn't wait to tell my friends."

She was not interested in settling down. "I always felt I would make my own success before I got married so I could bring something to the table," she reflects. As the lead singer with Irvin Charles and The Night Riders, a local band that opened for headliners like Bobby Blue Bland and Tina Turner, she had big plans.

Her velvety voice had won her first place in talent shows throughout high school and now she was ready to capitalize on her gift. She loved the limelight but when she started falling in love with Jim, she began to rethink her priorities. It was clear that she didn't have enough energy for the relationship and a singing career. She chose Jim.

When he got drafted for the Vietnam War the relationship shifted into high gear. "We had planned to get married anyway but that made us really step it up," Jim tells me. They drove around looking for a pastor who would marry them on short notice, and on the afternoon of March 20th, they became Mr. and Mrs. Edward Randall, Jr. Afterward they feasted on her mother's barbecue with family and friends.

From a big family, Mary had always been strong and independent. She liked the idea of supplementing her husband's income and tried everything from administrative work to a paper route before she deferred to his greater need—having a wife who stayed home with the children. "We had a plan and we worked it," Mary remembers. The plan included building themselves a home and putting money in the bank.

They settled into a comfortable routine. Every Friday night Jim took the family out to dinner and then met his friends for poker. At first she didn't worry about his gambling. Didn't he deserve a night out with the guys? Then one day she found the bank book and discovered that their savings was depleted.

"More and more he didn't want to go to parties or be with my friends," recalls Mary. "He started saying things like 'you're naggin'.' Seems like his whole theology was changing." He promised to quit but not before he had won back the money. As time went by, she began to lose hope and actually prayed that God would let her out of the marriage.

But God had something else in mind. "One day the Lord told me: *Stay with him. I'll make out of him everything you want him to be*." She didn't really believe it and still wanted to get out of the relationship: "I thought surely the Lord would reconsider."

Then one morning, after weeks of not speaking to each other, Mary and Jim had a conversation at the bathroom sink. "I know the only reason you're staying with me is 'cause the Lord told you to," he said to her. She almost choked on her toothpaste. She hadn't told a soul, so how could he know about her divine instructions? "I know you don't love me no more but you will," he continued. "Everything you want a husband and a man to be, I'm gonna be it. Wait and see."

At that moment, they recommitted themselves to each other and the marriage. Besides being filled with the desire to stay married, Jim was also blessed with a grateful heart. "Sometimes he'd wake me up at night and thank me for loving him enough to wrestle with him," says Mary. A man of few words, Jim never passes up an opportunity to give credit where it's due. "By the grace of God and Mary Randall, we made it."

Marriage is your last, best chance to grow up.

–Joseph Barth

Senator Bill and Sally (Sandlin) Ratliff

Wedding Date: August 8, 1959

We spent three or four hours a night just talking to each other.
—Bill Ratliff

It's Saturday morning and Bill and Sally Ratliff are drinking coffee in their downtown Austin apartment. Mount Pleasant is their permanent home but this comfy high-rise that overlooks the state capitol is where they hang their hats during the legislative session. Full of energy, Bill gets up several times to refill coffee cups and answer the phone while Sally answers questions about how they met. After a few minutes, he's telling the story, too.

It was 1958 and Sally was living at the Zeta Tau Alpha sorority house where Bill had come to pick up his cousin to take her home to El Dorado for the Thanksgiving weekend. Sitting on the floor playing bridge, Sally looked up as Bill came in to get his cousin's suitcase. She smiled at him with her big brown eyes. "I was smitten," he relates. "I don't know whether she knew it, but I was."

He called her as soon as he got back to town the following Sunday and they were together almost every day after that. She graduated the following year and moved to Big Spring for a teaching job. By Valentine's Day of 1959 he had had enough of that four-and-a-half-hour commute. He showed up on her doorstep with a box of chocolates and a marriage proposal. "She didn't give me an answer at first," he grins. "I should have given her a deadline."

Waiting for her reply, he knew one thing for sure. She wasn't after him for his money. "Back then, all I could spring for was hot chocolate," he laughs. "We spent three or four hours a night just talking to each other." Six months later, they were married in an

Episcopal ceremony in Mount Pleasant. Having grown up without a formal religion, he was baptized into her faith the day before the wedding. Money was tight those first years since he was finishing his degree and she couldn't find a full-time job. "Hard times early tend to make you appreciate what will come later." It also helped that they weren't the only ones in a tight situation. "All of our friends were in the same shape we were," says Sally. "That was before poor was identified."

As their family grew, so did his earning power, and Sally was able to stay ahead of the bills. At one point, she saved enough out of her household account to surprise him with a Rolex. Managing money was not a challenge for her but keeping up with his career changes was. "I have the absolute classic *seven-year itch*," he admits. "Every seven or eight years we've made a major change in our lives." She hasn't always been raring to go. "I guess the roughest time for her was when I yanked her up by the roots and moved her to Houston. She cried all the way down there."

"Actually, I cried all summer," adds Sally. Now she knows they did the right thing. "Those Houston years were very good to us. Without them, we wouldn't ever have been able to do what we're doing now."

He loves the way she keeps up with "his world." "I don't think there's another spouse in the legislature who comes over and sits in the gallery and just watches," he says. Sally shakes her head. To her it's no big deal. In fact, she can't imagine it any other way. "I know some women who aren't even aware of what their husband does all day. I couldn't live like that."

The hardest thing for her is dealing with Bill's tunnel vision—his way of blocking out everything else when he's working on a project. "Back when he was redoing school finance, I told him I was going to take the computer and drop kick it out the window."

Bill says that, at first, he had trouble interpreting her emotional signals. "The first time that Sally cried, I thought the marriage was over," says Bill, who grew up with two brothers. "I just wasn't used to people crying. I'm not good at sensitive subjects or talking about emotions."

He's learning. Meanwhile, she's picking up a thing or two about the economy of words. "He can say it in about ten words," she tells me. "It takes me a day and a half."

All in all, they're pretty good at figuring out what the other one needs. "Sally's favorite thing in all the world is just to walk down a beach," Bill says. "I have to get her to the saltwater once a year or I'm afraid she'll curl up and die." Whether it's a week at La Jolla, or an afternoon in Port Aransas, they usually celebrate Valentine's Day with their feet in the sand. "We do stupid things," she confides, "like see who can find the most sand dollars."

Seldom or perhaps never does a marriage develop into an individual relationship smoothly and without crises; there is no coming to consciousness without pain.

–Carl Jung

Darrell and Edith (Thomason) Royal

Wedding Date: July 26, 1944

Don't try to change anybody to fit what you want them to be.
—Edith Royal

In 1942, when Edith Marie Thomason met Darrell Royal, she had never seen a football game and he had never had a girlfriend. They soon made up for any lack of experience.

She was in her sophomore year at the public high school in Gould, Oklahoma, when a friend of hers invited her to a high school football game in nearby Hollis. She was happy to meet the blue-eyed quarterback named Darrell Royal but, unlike most of the other girls, she wasn't awed by the star of the team. "I didn't know enough about football to be impressed. But he was shy and I liked that. I thought that would be a challenge."

The courtship had been going for over a year when Uncle Sam called Darrell into service. "He asked me to keep his football jacket," she remembers. "I thought he'd come back for the jacket even if he didn't come back for me."

Darrell was a bit more confident. "I knew I wanted to marry her about a year after we met," he says. "But we never talked about it until I had a reporting date for the service. The day before I had to report for duty in Lawton, Oklahoma, we both brought it up. I remember she had on a polka dot dress.

"It was one of those marriages destined for failure. I had nothing but my ass and my hat. Statistics dictate that we should have waited."

"But it was war time," explains Edith. "Nobody waited because you never knew whether you'd see each other after that next shipping out."

She finished high school and was working at an army base near Oklahoma City while he finished his training at Will Rogers field.

One day, with very little planning, they took the plunge. "We just went up and knocked on the preacher's door and we had the license, so he married us," says Darrell.

Edith was eighteen and Darrell was twenty that hot Saturday morning in the summer of '44 when they walked the short distance from Edith's apartment to the First United Methodist Church in Oklahoma City. During a simple ceremony, they promised their undying love in front of the minister and an air force buddy and his girlfriend.

After a brief honeymoon in Hollis, Darrell reported back to Will Rogers Field where, as the starting quarterback for the Third Air Force, he began to concentrate on football. After pondering over scholarship offers from the Citadel, Florida, Alabama, USC, Texas Tech, Georgia, South Carolina, Tennessee, Cornell, Auburn, and the University of Detroit, he accepted one from the University of Oklahoma.

Meanwhile, Edith concentrated on starting their family and pretty soon baby Marian was sharing that little one-bedroom rent house. In Darrell's mind, making ends meet was a huge challenge and he gives Edith every bit of the credit for getting them through it. "She had to really, really scrimp," he recalls. "I look back and don't see how we did it."

Edith doesn't remember it that way. "It was no struggle," she says, shaking her head. "It was easy. Every afternoon, I'd dress up the kids and stroll them down to the campus corner drugstore. We'd meet Darrell and drink chocolate malts and fool around. We had a good time."

Meanwhile his accomplishments on the University of Oklahoma football field were being splashed across the sports pages of the newspaper with increasing regularity. By the time Edith delivered their second child, her husband was a local celebrity. As she watched her husband take center stage she settled happily into her supporting role. Playing second fiddle didn't bother her at all. "She was an excellent coach's wife," says Darrell. "I had eight jobs in eight years. She never hesitated to move and she never complained. A lot of the wives complained, but not Edith."

In her mind there was nothing to complain about. "I think the key was that I was as excited as he was. I felt very much a part of things, like a teammate. I knew my job was important—to take care of everything else so he could do what he needed to do."

It wasn't until years later that they experienced rough waters when two of their three children were taken from them. Their daughter was killed in an automobile accident while in her twenties and several years later their son died in a motorcycle crash. These sudden and devastating losses did not bring them closer together. "After the deaths of our children we grieved in separate ways, in different ways," says Edith. "His way was to keep busy and go places . . . to be with lots of people. I needed to be alone. We could not comfort each other so we almost broke up."

With the help of a twelve-step program, she found a way to give him the space he needed. Now she believes that learning how to be apart may have been what kept them together. She realizes that what worked for them won't work for everyone but there is one piece of wisdom that applies to us all. "Don't try to change anybody to fit what you want them to be," she says. "It only took me forty years to figure that out. I finally told Darrell, 'I'm not coachable.'"

Darrell listens as Edith talks, watching her with those intense blue eyes of his. He has no interest in analyzing their married life. Let somebody else figure out the formula for a perfect relationship. All he knows is he's one lucky guy to have spent his life with a woman like Edith. He may not see himself as the romantic type, but he sure sounds poetic when he talks about the only woman he's ever loved.

"You know that song—*The Wind Beneath My Wings*?" he asks. "That's Edith. She's the wind beneath my wings."

Hyman and Louise (Anderson) Samuelson

Wedding Date: September 19, 1945

It was kind of a practical thing.
—Hyman Samuelson

Louise Anderson Samuelson smiles when she thinks about meeting her husband for the first time. "I took one look and said *This is mine. This is mine.* Poor boy, he didn't know if he was coming or going." She decided the way to his heart was through his stomach. "I found out all his favorite foods and cooked them," she remembers. "I finally snared him after three months."

An army captain accustomed to eating in the mess hall, Hyman welcomed her frequent dinner invitations but romance was the last thing on his mind. "My relationship with Louise was anything but romantic. It was kind of a practical thing. I needed somebody to take care of my little boy."

He was still grieving his wife who had died of cancer just a few months before. Since that time, three-year-old Ian had been living with his grandmother and Hyman was determined to get him back. It was a task that proved more difficult than he had anticipated. "I didn't know quite how to get him back from her," he recalls. "There was a strong emotional attachment. The only way to do it was to come home with a wife."

Honest to a fault, he told Louise exactly how he felt about her when he proposed. "I should tell you I love you first but I don't know whether I do or not," he said. Louise, who also had a young son to support, didn't think a thing of the fact that he had an ulterior motive. "It didn't bother me," she says with a shrug. "Didn't bother me in the least. I knew I loved Hymie and that was good enough."

In September of 1945 they got married at the

home of a justice of the peace in Olympia, Washington, where Louise had lived her entire life. Hyman was tall, dark, and dashing in his captain's uniform and she was small, blonde, and beautiful in a light green suit. They exchanged vows in front of their two sons and Hyman's parents.

Then the foursome headed south for New Orleans, Hyman's birthplace and where most of his family still lived. It seemed like a good place to start over but it wasn't. "I tried to establish roots again in New Orleans but I couldn't. I had a lot of old girlfriends there, I had family. Suddenly I found myself with a wife and two kids. That wasn't exactly what I wanted, either. I didn't know what the hell I wanted."

They checked out Houston, Galveston, and Lake Charles before settling in Austin where Hyman and his cousin opened a clothing store. In the short time since he'd finished his tour of duty, he'd become a husband, father, and a small business owner. Things were going well.

Then, on Christmas day of 1946, life took a tragic turn. Little Ian was killed in a freak automobile accident. Tears fill his eyes as he tells what happened. "My father drove into the bumper of a car parked in front of the house and the car rolled into the yard," he says. "It hit my little boy and killed him."

It almost killed the marriage as well. "I had married Louise to help me with my child. Now my child was gone. I didn't know just how I felt. It was bad."

A few months later when Louise delivered their first child, he was still grief stricken and had no desire to get attached to the infant. In fact, he did everything he could to keep his distance. "I did not want to love that little baby," he admits, his voice trembling. "It looked like everything I loved died. I didn't want to have much to do with her."

Since the baby was small and sickly and Louise couldn't do it all by herself, he started pitching in. With every bottle he gave her, the tiny little thing made off with another piece of his heart. Louise gives their daughter credit for rescuing the relationship. "Becky saved the marriage," she says. "Suddenly, we had something else to put our minds on."

After that they had two more children and along the way, Louise converted to Judaism. Over the years, she has always put Hyman's needs first. He says he's never spent more than a moment being angry with her. She can't say the same thing, however, remembering how much it used to hurt when he'd leave her and the children on Sunday afternoons to go off and write in his journal.

And then there was his strong interest in other women. "Women are important to me," he explains. "I'm not going to bed with them, but I love to talk to them and I write to a lot of women."

She accepted the fact that his intentions were honorable. "When my friends asked 'Aren't you jealous?' I said, 'Of what? I'm the one he's going home with.'"

These days they are like two little kids in a candy store. "When we drive to Houston together for a wedding or something, we giggle the whole way," she says.

"Although I did not love Louise when I married her, I adore her now," he says reaching for her hand. Louise is not surprised. "I knew I could bring him around."

> *Rejoice in the wife of your youth. Let her charms and tender embrace satisfy you. Let her love alone fill you with delight.*
>
> –Proverbs 5:18-19

Louis and Caroline (Cattarusa) Sanchez

Wedding Date: February 21, 1934

Rudy and Pauline (Sanchez) Villarreal

Wedding Date: November 21, 1954

A Salt-of-the-Earth Foursome
Made of Two "Texas Twosomes"

When it comes to meeting the challenges of married life, the Villarreals have an unfair advantage. Ideal role models live right next door. With sixty plus years behind them, Caroline and Louis Sanchez are pretty sure they're going to make it. The two couples live in an oak studded section of northwest San Antonio where their yards are connected by a wrought iron fence and a welcoming gate. Pretty as it is, the gate rarely gets used since these people have more of a "come on in, the back door's open" kind of relationship. No question about it, these couples are close. You might even say they are bonded for life. Caroline and Louis are Pauline's parents.

Pauline and Rudy have been married since 1954. Louis and Caroline, since 1934. With 108 wedding anniversaries between them, they know a few things about getting along and are learning more from each other all the time. They watch football in the fall and fish for mackerel in the summer. Last year the "kids" bought a new van to drive their parents to the coast.

It would take a page to list the things they have in common, but most important of all is the way they look at marriage. Here's the scoop on "Mom and Dad."

Louis and Caroline's Story

We always prayed and had faith in God.
—Caroline Sanchez

"We grew up in the same neighborhood," says Louis from his overstuffed chair in the living room. He's definitely the talker of the two, turning to Caroline every so often for verification. She nods her head and waits to tell her story.

Born in Italy, Caroline came to America at the age of four when her parents died. She moved in with her Uncle Frank who made his living in the grocery business. By the age of ten, she was stocking shelves; by sixteen she was making deliveries. When she first came to the Sanchez house, she was loaded down with a week's worth of groceries. She met everybody in the family but Louis that first day. He was still at work. A few weeks later, he drove over to the school and introduced himself.

"He picked me up from school one day and that was it," says Caroline, her dark eyes shining. She remembers that he was a standout on the amateur boxing circuit and she found his muscles quite appealing. She also liked the fact that other girls liked him. "He was popular," she recalls. "That was one attraction." He laughs and says he proposed to her to keep her from running off with someone else. "She always had a bunch of boys who liked her."

It helped that they were both Catholic, since marrying outside the faith was strongly discouraged in those days. After a proper courtship, he asked Uncle Frank for her hand. She was sixteen. It was 1932 and because of the Great Depression they had a simple church wedding with no honeymoon. They weren't used to luxuries anyway, so they settled right down to the business of starting a family. Louis wanted Caroline to stay home with their children. That was fine with her. After working half her life, she was ready to be a full-time homemaker.

Their first son died of pneumonia at six months of age. Infant deaths were more common in those days. "We went to church a lot," she says. That's how they coped with most of the hardships they encountered.

Shortly after the baby died, they had Pauline, then another daughter and, finally, another son. "The babies came boom, boom, boom," she said. In 1943, Louis shipped out to the Philippines, leaving her and their two, four, and six-year-old children in the care of his mother and Uncle Frank. The next two years were long. "We walked to my mother-in-law's house every Saturday," says Caroline. Ever since Louis came back from the war in 1945, they haven't spent a night apart. His philosophy is that just

being together goes a long way in strengthening a marriage. "You can't have a good marriage without spending time together." He also thinks couples should avoid excessive alcohol. "We all like to drink a little but taken to a degree it can make you fuss and leave home."

She recommends that couples put their trust in the Lord. It's an attitude that has served them well. "We always prayed and had faith in God."

God the best maker of all marriages,
combined your hearts in one.
–William Shakespeare

Rudy and Pauline's Story

Whenever we had a little fight,
I'd think about my wedding vows.
—PAULINE VILLARREAL

Pauline and Rudy grew up in the same neighborhood, too. His mother sewed dresses for her and her sister when they were little, and Pauline ran around with Rudy's younger sister in high school. She didn't actually meet her future husband until he came back from the Korean War in the early 1950s. He remembers when he first saw seventeen-year-old Pauline Sanchez, standing in her front yard. She was the sweetest sight he'd ever seen. He started making up excuses to walk past her house. She noticed the tall air force corporal hanging around but didn't know why he kept staring at her. One day she came right out and asked him.

"What are you looking at so much?"

"At you," he replied.

That was the right answer. Before long they were going to the movies and the amusement park every week. It was a rather formal courtship complete with 9:00 P.M. curfew and fifteen-year-old chaperone; her little sister tagged along to ride the roller coaster. Pauline says they were having a great time but she was eager to move on to the next stage. One night he came over and she popped the question.

"Do you intend to marry me someday?" she asked.

"Yes," he replied.

"Okay, I'm going on a trip to California next week. I want my ring."

That was that. Several months later they got married in a Catholic church and like her mother and father, they immediately began working on their family. Unlike her mother and father, for them children didn't come easily. Many years went by and still no baby. "That was hard," she admits. "I still don't know why I never got pregnant. The doctor said there was no reason why I couldn't."

Rudy would not let her give up hope and he comforted her with his confidence. "We prayed every day," he says. "I told her that a baby would come. Don't worry, I said, everything is going to be all right."

They kept a crib in their spare bedroom and babysat for anyone who asked them. After ten years of crying, waiting, and wondering, she got pregnant. They finally had their miracle. "I couldn't believe it," she says, her eyes bright with the memory. "She was Rudy's joy." Seven years later, she delivered a second baby girl.

Waiting for children had been hard. It brought stress and arguments, but Pauline had a special exercise that helped get her

through it. "Whenever we had a little fight or something I'd think of my wedding vows. I don't know why, I just did. My wedding vows meant a lot to me."

She reaches over and pats his hand. "I think I've had one heck of a life with him. He does everything for me."

He has always known what to say to make her feel better. "I tell her, don't worry. Everything's gonna be all right."

> *Love does not consist in gazing at each other*
> *but in looking outward together in the same direction.*
>
> –Antoine de Saint-Exupery

Luke and Mary (Varisco) Scamardo

Wedding Date: January 12, 1922

You gotta try to live that promise.
—Luke Scamardo

Mary Varisco was seventeen years old when her brother introduced her to the handsome Italian man outside the Catholic church in Bryan, Texas. Aside from the fact that Luke was eight years older, they had a lot in common, having both immigrated to Texas from the same small town in Italy when they were very young. Sitting at their kitchen table almost seventy-five years later, just a few miles from where they met, they are thinking about what attracted them to each other. "I fell for him right away," she says. "He was neat looking, you know?"

She isn't accustomed to talking about her feelings, and every once in a while she turns her head and blushes. Luke, on the other hand, doesn't have a shy bone in his body. His hearing may be on it's way out but his memory is strong as ever. "I looked her over real good," he says. "I thought she was the best looking woman in the world."

Dating was different in those days. Parents didn't let their youngsters go out alone and so most of the courting took place in the girl's parlor. When Luke decided he wanted Mary, he went to her father first and it was Mr. Varisco who did the asking. "I had another boy at the time who wanted to marry me," she remembers. "My daddy asked me which one I'd like to marry and I told him Luke. I liked his ways."

Not one to let an opportunity slip by, Luke also asked his prospective father-in-law for permission to run the family grocery store. He must have really charmed Mr. Varisco because he ended up with his daughter and his business, and was also invited to move into their house. Intended as a way to save commuting time, it turned out to be a good way to get to know the bride before the wedding. "He lived with us, my brothers, my parents and me," says Mary. "That's exactly the way it was."

With all those chaperones, was there any chance of sneaking a kiss before the wedding?

"Of course not," she says, her face turning red.

"Well, sure," he said, grinning ear to ear.

They pledged their love in the winter of 1922 when he slipped a small ruby ring on her finger at St. Joseph's Catholic Church. Afterward, there was a celebration at her parents' house that lasted for days. "People drank and ate all night long," she recalls. "My parents emptied a bedroom to make room for dancing. I was worn out."

With no money for a honeymoon, they went back to work in the grocery store the very next day. Mary continued to run the cash register even after the babies started coming. "I had three children but to tell you the truth, mostly my mother and my sister took care of them," she confides. "I was lucky to live so close to my mother and daddy."

Luke and Mary lived their whole life on the land they bought in the 30s, in the same ranch-style house where they reared their children. For the past couple of years, they've mostly stayed at home, watching soap operas and puttering around the house. He loves the fancy recliner she bought him last Christmas, but she sometimes misses their busy social calendar. "We used to have friends over to our house all the time but all our friends have died now," she laments. "We used to go to town and the movies every week. He never went without me."

After seventy-five years with the same woman, Luke now spends his days trying to figure out how to get along without her. She died in her sleep recently at the age of ninety-two. Though he misses her terribly, he counts himself among the lucky ones for the kind of marriage they enjoyed for almost seventy-six years. Along the way, he learned a thing or two about how to keep the bond. "Anytime you have something in mind you want to do and it's not good, think of the promise you made to God when you married her," he says. "That you would live together forever until death do you part. The promise is for good and bad times. You gotta try to live that promise."

Love is all we have, the only way
that each can help each other.

–Euripides

Neil and Lynn (Noecker) Sperry

Wedding Date: August 6, 1967

You can't give up every time it gets rocky.
—LYNN SPERRY

The Dallas Arboretum seemed like a good place to interview Texas' best known gardener and his wife of more than thirty-one years. That's where we hooked up with Neil and Lynn Sperry on a Sunday afternoon in late July. Even with the temperature up around 100 degrees, they couldn't wait to show us around, pointing out coneflowers and lantanas as we walked along. In search of a cooler spot, we invaded the volunteer office, where the lady in charge recognized Neil and showed us to a room where the Sperrys could tell their story.

They met in 1965 at Ohio State University where he was pursuing a degree in horticulture and she was studying music. On Mother's Day they both ended up at the Student Union for the Alpha Zeta family brunch where Lynn's brother introduced them. The very next week she had her brother ask Neil if he might like to go out. "I was premature," she explains. "Women weren't asking back then." He turned her down, saying that he already had a girlfriend back in College Station.

However, by the time he got home for the summer, the girlfriend was history. He immediately thought of Lynn. "What I noticed about her then is the same thing I notice about her today and every day since. She is a warm and wholesome person. The kind you would like to marry. I've never been attracted to glitzy or flashy people."

After they had been dating for a while, he graduated and went to Colorado State for a master's degree. When she visited him over spring break, he offered her his fraternity pin. This time, she was the one who declined. "I wasn't going back to Ohio State

pinned to some guy in Colorado and have my social life finished," she says.

It was time for the full court press. That summer he found her a one-month job and a place to stay in Fort Collins. They worked at a restaurant together during the week and biked through the lush Colorado countryside on the weekends. He spent his last $300 to buy her a ring. "We got engaged," he recalls. "She was willing to accept a diamond ring."

They married in the summer of 1967 after their mutual attraction had developed into deep affection. Neil is candid about their chemistry. "I can honestly say, and I don't think it hurts her feelings, I wasn't head over heels in love and neither was she," he admits. "But we both love each other very dearly and, to this day, I am very sad when she's gone for a weekend or whatever. It's a mature relationship. When I married, I had the feeling that I was going to stay married forever."

Same with her. "I was brought up in the church to think that marriage is a one shot deal. The mindset that you bring to your marriage is important. If you say 'Oh well, I can always get a divorce' when times get tough, then you won't try as hard. You can't give up every time it gets rocky."

Like the day their seventeen-year-old daughter confessed that she had a problem with drugs. "We discovered that we had a cocaine addict in our house on October 31, 1995, Tuesday night at 7:00," he remembers, as if it happened yesterday. "After we found out about Erin, we went out and had our favorite hamburger. We didn't cry, we didn't scream. We said, 'Well, what do we do now?'"

Since then, they've cried a lot. But with the help of the Families Anonymous twelve-step program they've learned how to get through it. "The motto is *Let go and let God*," says Lynn. "Sometimes we have to rely on somebody bigger than we are."

"If there is a message we can impart to other couples with children it's this one," Neil says, "We didn't cause Erin's problems and we can't cure them." Lynn isn't quite as eager to share their experience but Neil wants to tell anyone who might benefit from their life travels. "We've had struggles with business. We've had struggles with children," he confides, "and there are issues that continue to go on in our lives . . . But we've survived those and our marriage has gotten better with each year. I just think that's the process of maturing into a marriage."

Most of all, it takes time, he says. "One of the most important things in marriage is patience."

Love is like quicksilver in the hand. Leave the fingers open and it stays. Clutch it and it darts away.

–Dorothy Parker

Roger and Marianne (Hoobler) Staubach

Wedding Date: September 4, 1965

Throughout your marriage you have to keep choosing to love that person.
—Marianne Staubach

"Jolly Roger Takes a Mate." That was the headline on the front page of the Cincinnati paper the morning after Roger Staubach and Marianne Hoobler got married. The photo showed them leaving the cathedral beneath the crossed swords of naval officers in their dress whites. It was a storybook wedding that friends and family will never forget. "We were both from middle class, hard-working families," says Roger. "The wedding was a big deal because of the Naval Academy and my athletic career, else it probably would have been a small one."

It was also a big deal because the bride and groom had known each other since fourth grade, although they admit the relationship didn't really get rolling until the eighth grade. That's when the basketball players and cheerleaders started riding together to the off-campus games. When the nuns ushered the students into taxicabs with the girls ending up on the guys' laps, it was a turning point in Roger's life. He realized there was more to life than competitive sports. "Marianne was cute," he says. "She was a cheerleader. I kinda migrated towards the cheerleaders."

They went on to different high schools but kept getting together for dances and proms. "But we never went steady," she explains. By the time he finished Annapolis, she was a registered nurse. That's when they decided to get married. Fourteen years seemed a long enough courtship. "I think you have to have some qualities that are similar and we do," she says. "Even though Roger is an only child and I'm one of five, we grew up in the same type of family circumstances. And, of course, there's our Catholic faith."

It's a warm summer evening at their vacation home on Lake LBJ. A fiery sun is glistening on the grey green water and

Marianne and Roger are talking about what marriage means to them. "You always have a friend," she says, "Someone to share with. There's somebody there when something good happens or when you need someone to support you and comfort you."

She's thinking of those days after the death of their fourth child, who was delivered stillborn. Roger made sure all the baby things were put away before she came home from the hospital. Marianne appreciates him. "He takes care of me. He has always taken care of me."

They didn't discuss it beforehand but Marianne always knew she wanted to stay home with her children. It was what her mother had done and it seemed right for her, too. Roger, whose mother went back to work when he was still young, said he would've been happy either way. "If Marianne wanted a different way of life, I would adjust to that . . . You just can't dominate your spouse. But she has always wanted to be in the home. Running a home with five children is a big deal."

Being supportive works both ways. "I'm not stupid. I know if I'm nice to her it can be a good thing for me. And you can't turn it off and on. You can't be a couple of jerks running around and then all of a sudden want to have a physical relationship. Commitment is a big part of it.You have to have a relationship that's going on all the time to make sure you live up to that commitment. It's got to be an ongoing process."

Faithfulness is a given for Roger. "I'm confused at how some people love each other so much but they don't have the faithfulness that goes with it." Most of their differences seem to be basic to men and women. "It's a typical thing. Women want details. I want to know who he had lunch with and that kind of stuff. But that's not really important to him," says Marianne.

According to Roger, intimacy requires good communication. "Marianne knows more about me than anyone. Still, I'm an only child. I tend to keep a lot inside. I don't think any marriage has enough communication."

Whether they are birds of a feather or opposites attracting, they admit to having widened their horizons since they've been together. Says Marianne, "He exposed me to a lot of things that I probably would have never pursued on my own. I probably wouldn't even have this fitness trainer except for the fact that he's always been into physical fitness. In return, I don't think he would ever have gone to a play."

"You've got to have flexibility in a marriage," Roger agrees. "If you don't, you'll never make it. I'm hard-headed as can be. Sometimes she has to sit me down and say 'that's not the way it's going to be.'"

They believe that love is a choice you make. "Throughout marriage you have to keep choosing to love that person," Marianne offers. She also had to learn to give him space, especially when their house was full of teenagers and he, having retired from the Cowboys, was spending long hours at the office. "He just really needed 'down time,'" she recalls. "He didn't want to answer a lot of questions all the time."

With five grown children to keep up with and a demanding social calendar, their latest challenge has been finding time for each other. They sit down at the kitchen table every few weeks and compare Daytimers. "It was important for me not to take for granted that Marianne would be available," he confesses. She smiles at him and her green eyes light up.

"Roger has come a long way with that."

> *Marriage is an act of will that signifies*
> *and involves a mutual gift . . .*
>
> –Pope John Paul II (b. 1920)

ED.
STEVENS

Eddie and Margie (Saxon) Stevens

Wedding Date: April 16, 1943

If a ball player doesn't have a wife who loves baseball, he might as well get out.
—Eddie Stevens

Sitting beside her husband on the cedar chest he gave her for a wedding present, she giggles and pats his knee. "I just can't believe we've been married this long."

Eddie and Margie Stevens are in the study of their southwest Houston home surrounded by baseball memorabilia. Pictures, jerseys, and home run balls reflect a career that has spanned more than four decades. Sometimes a blessing, sometimes a curse, they have fond memories of their baseball life.

It was 1943 when native Galvestonian Eddie Stevens first met Margie Saxon—the youngest of six army brats living in Meadeville, Mississippi. They were introduced by Eddie's cousin who had been raving about Margie for weeks. Eddie fell in love with the enthusiastic sixteen-year-old almost immediately. "She was a nice looking young girl . . . personable, full of energy. I just finally told her I was going to take her on home with me."

Without any formal training, she learned how to nurse his baseball fever. "Some women just weren't cut out to be baseball wives," he says. "But Margie was. She loved it."

The romance began when seventeen-year-old Eddie was playing pro ball with a Class D West Texas league. Every week he'd ride the bus from Galveston to Meadeville. If his bus got to town before Margie's classes were over, he hung out in the hallways just waiting for her. The tall, blue-eyed boy was welcomed by the faculty. "The high school librarian was real sweet," says Margie. "She let us court in the library." In April of 1943 they said "I do" in front of a Baptist preacher, the preacher's wife, and

Margie's mother. It was a busy day for the bride. "We were married at 3:00 in the afternoon and I graduated high school that night," says Margie, her blue eyes twinkling.

They left for Texas that same night so Eddie could register for the draft. However, flat feet kept him out of the service and he immediately went back to doing what he loved best—playing first base and hitting the long ball. During his second year of marriage, he climbed up from Class D to Triple A ball and went through spring training with the Brooklyn Dodgers. "I couldn't believe they would give me money to play baseball," he recalls.

The euphoria quickly faded into life on the road. "The hardest thing was on Margie. She had to load up the kids and drive everywhere I was playing. It was a lot of responsibility." Margie shakes her head. "That's just the way it was. I thought nothing of hitting the road with those children." Once she led a caravan from Daytona Beach, Florida, to Rochester, New

York. "Some of the wives were terrified," she remembers. "But I wasn't afraid, it was just what I had to do. By the time Eddie joined us, I had unpacked all the boxes and made cookies." Over the years she made homes for Eddie and their three daughters in Brooklyn, Indianapolis, San Diego, Rochester, Toronto, and Montreal. "It was fun," she says. "It was our way of life."

Meanwhile, most of Eddie's teammates were falling victim to the growing divorce rate. Watching the marriages around him dissolve, he developed a simple philosophy: "If a ball player doesn't have a wife who loves baseball, he might as well get out. If she will back him 100 percent then he will dedicate more time and attention to her."

In 1947 he had the second best record for home runs and RBI. Ironically, that's when the manager asked him to give up his position. He remembers the conversation perfectly. "Mr. Rickey asked me to go back to Montreal and make room for Jackie Robinson. He said if I had myself a good year that he would bring me back and I'd have a job for the next ten, fifteen years, as long as my ability would allow me. We shook hands in a gentlemen's agreement."

Eddie kept his end of the bargain, leading his Triple A team in home runs, RBI, runs scored, and extra base hits that season. Unfortunately, the Dodgers brought him back up three days too late to qualify for the 1947 World Series. The next winter, they traded him to Pittsburgh.

Then Eddie got sick. Forty-nine doctors and four years later, he was diagnosed with an infection. By the time he recovered, his reputation was shot. "All the ballclubs were saying 'you're still a good ballplayer and you can do the job, but you're a cripple and we can't take you back,'" Eddie recalls.

So he traded his bat for a clipboard and stopwatch and began another career as a professional baseball scout—another version of life on the road. "Baseball was our life, our livelihood. That was what he loved to do," says Margie. "I never once asked him to get out of baseball."

There were other hardships. In the late '80s their son-in-law was murdered, and after that one of their daughters suffered a stroke. "What saw us through—we've always been Christian, we've always relied on our faith," Margie says. "We go to church three times a week."

Eddie wishes today's athletes had the same values: "The thing lacking in professional sports today is dedication and loyalty. You could apply that to marriage, too. You've got to keep that faith and trust in each other no matter what. You have to keep the faith."

She commandeth her husband, in any equal matter,
by constantly obeying him.

–Thomas Fuller, 1608-1661

C. J. and Gudelia (Villasana) Villegas

Wedding Date: September 11, 1945

I say save your energy ladies,
let him be the boss.
—GUDELIA VILLEGAS

When Gudelia talks about her life with C. J., it is clear that she has either a very good marriage or a very bad memory. "I don't remember ever struggling or suffering," she says. "I look back and say what's the big deal about staying married."

We're sitting at a table in El Mercado, their family-owned Mexican restaurant in South Austin. With an eye on the lunch crowd, they're thinking back on the days when they first got together.

Gudelia was a fourteen-year-old teenager giggling with her girlfriends at the neighborhood recreation center when she first saw C. J. Even at seventeen, it didn't take him long to make up his mind about her. "I liked her right away," he recalls. "I knew she had a boyfriend but I also knew I could steal her away."

With frequent phone calls and front porch visits, that's exactly what he set out to do. Replacing her boyfriend was easy; coping with her protective father wasn't. Since Gudelia's mother died when she was ten, her dad was rearing his daughters alone. He was totally committed to the task of keeping boys away.

"Her dad was real strict," remembers C. J. "I'd come over to her house when he was gone and we'd sit on the porch and talk. Then I'd have to leave early because he'd come home and be mad. I had to sneak in and sneak out."

Soon after her fifteenth birthday they grew weary of trying to hide their feelings. Jumping into his Model A, they drove to San Marcos and with a $10 license, got married by a justice of the peace. They

spent their five-day honeymoon right there.

"We were hiding out," jokes Gudelia.

Camillo is not proud of the way they handled it. "We lied about our ages to get blood tests. We got married before we even had a place to live."

In spite of everything, there were no postnuptial regrets and it wasn't long before that one-room efficiency began to feel like home. She spent her days decorating, cooking, and cleaning while he fixed engines at an automotive repair shop. It was three months before C. J. worked up the nerve to visit his father-in-law.

"Who are you?" barked Mr. Villasana when he saw the young man standing at his door. Swallowing hard, C. J. explained that he loved his new wife and was quite capable of providing for her and their future family. Ultimately, the older man forgave him. That meant a lot to C. J., whose own father died when he was young.

The newlyweds ended up moving into an apartment behind the

Villasana's grocery store and the two men soon became friends. Family was important to both of them. Soon after they bought a home for themselves, C. J. and Gudelia bought a home for his mother right next door.

That made things easier for Gudelia when her husband went off to Pennsylvania for a three-month training course. "Sometimes his mother came to help me with the children," she says. "We did what we had to do."

When they had been married for eighteen years, C. J. was laid off quite suddenly. It was a desperate situation for a man with seven mouths to feed. He drove over to his father-in-law's taco factory to give Gudelia the bad news and the next thing he knew he was working there too, repairing machines for a dollar an hour.

Both Hispanic and Catholic, they had quite a bit in common, but that doesn't mean that they didn't have conflicts. C. J. played the drums for a small band that often performed in clubs around town. Once, after he had been out making music the night before, she got a phone call from a friend informing her that C. J. had been dancing with other women during his breaks. Gudelia was not pleased at the thought of her husband in the arms of another woman while she was home caring for their children.

Before he could explain, she threw herself at him with all the strength her 100-pound frame could muster. She ranted and raved and flailed her arms and all he could say was, "it was only a dance." Still unsure about what he'd done wrong, he promised it would never happen again.

Believe it or not, that's the only real fight she can remember. "There's only one boss," says Gudelia. "Maybe some couples have troubles because they both want to be the boss. I guess I don't have any women's lib in me but I say 'Save your energy ladies, let him be the boss.'"

Marriage resembles a pair of shears, so joined that they cannot be separated, often moving in opposite directions yet always punishing anyone who comes between them.

–Sydney Smith

Danny and Lu (Helberg) Young

Wedding Date: July 6, 1965

I want it to go on forever.
–Danny Young

Before settling in for a talk with Danny and Lu Young, we take a tour of their home. Near Zilker Park in South Austin, this house means a lot to them since they've poured so much of themselves into it. He hung antique doors and installed wooden floors in the living room. She laid a brick patio in the backyard and planted an herb garden. Together, they built a greenhouse out of recycled wood.

Pointing to the wallpaper in the hallway, Danny beams. "This is one of the sure signs of a great marriage: Lu and I hung this wallpaper together. If you can wallpaper together and stay married, you know you have a good thing." She looks up at him as if he was crazy. "Honest to God, Danny, I can't remember you lifting one finger to help with this wallpaper." Then they both laugh. It's not uncommon for them to see things from different perspectives. Lu says the important thing is that they share the same world view.

They were both born in northwestern Ohio, but Danny's family moved to Kingsville, Texas, when he was about ten. Lu's brother Lee, who is sixteen years older than she is, married one of Danny's aunts. When they started having children, Lu became their babysitter. She met Danny while accompanying her brother's family to a Young wedding in Dallas. Danny was twenty-two when he first saw his future wife. "She got out of the car with that beautiful blonde hair. She was about twenty, I guess and she just knocked me out."

They enjoyed each other's company that weekend but it wasn't earth shattering for either of them. As soon as the wedding festivities were over, he returned to his duties with the Coast Guard on the Olympic Peninsula and she went back to her studies at Michigan State University. However, on her way home, Lu got a glimpse of things to come. "Sis and I stopped at my aunt and uncle's house in Texarkana on the drive back to Ohio," she recalls. "I told my aunt about meeting Danny and she cried. She said something about it being 'meant to be.' I can't really remember her exact words."

"I can," Danny interjects. "Her exact words were 'You're going to marry him.'

The next time they saw each other was a year and a half later at his grandparents' fiftieth anniversary party in Ohio. This time they spent about a week and a half together. "I just couldn't get enough of her," Danny says. "I was nuts about her from that point on." The first time he sat in the front seat of her Rambler, he realized they were meant to be. "She had her radio tuned to WLAC out of Nashville, my favorite station. I was from South Texas and she was from northwestern Ohio but we listened to the same station. What are the chances?"

A couple of years after they met, he was assigned to a year of isolated duty in the Bering Sea, but before going, he had to complete a training course in advanced electronics in Connecticut. After buying a wedding ring, he made a detour on his drive east. "I went to Ohio and proposed to her in the living room of my grandparents' house," he says. They were married in the Methodist church in New London, Connecticut, on July 6, 1965. Two sailors from his electronics class served as witnesses. After a short period of time together, he was shipped out. She went to live with her folks in Ohio for the next twelve months while awaiting the birth of their son. Scott Young was three months old before Danny ever saw him.

It was a difficult year. Only one experience has been harder and that was Lu's battle against cancer. Now she's in remission, but between 1994 and 1997 she underwent extensive radiation and chemotherapy. It was painful for her and terrifying for him. "Are you familiar with the passage in the Bible where you walk through the valley of the shadow of death?" he asks. "I'm supposed to take care of this woman and, other than just holding the pan, there wasn't a damn thing I could do."

She thought he did plenty. "He was wonderful. Everything else in his life was second to helping me."

Danny likes his wife's sense of independence. "She knows exactly what it is that she wants out of life and where she's going with it . . . I don't like clingy, dependent women. I like those strong Texas women who say, 'Okay, if you don't like it, to hell with you!'"

Lu says many things have changed over the past thirty-three years. "We had the same sort of disagreements early on that most people do. I remember one time he got really mad because there was no sugar in the house. We don't do that anymore. If you want sugar, you go and buy it." Danny says their promise goes beyond the two of them. "I made a vow to God that I would love this woman forsaking all others until death do us part. I want it to go on forever."

Love is much like a wild rose, beautiful and calm
but willing to draw blood in its defense.

–Mark Overby

The following pages
are provided
for your own
"*Twosome*"
story.

Place your
photograph
here

Aye, you shall be together even in the silent memory of God.
But let there by spaces in your togetherness,
And let the winds of the heavens dance between you . . .

–Kahlil Gibran, the Prophet